"When I lie awake through the night watches, I earnestly pray for friends who are suffering greatly. I ask God to stretch their tolerance for pain, stoke the smoking embers of their hopes, and to build in them a rugged, more sturdy faith. And now, I have this excellent guide, *I'm Praying for You*, to assist me with my intercessions. I couldn't be more thrilled, for my good friend Nancy Guthrie has filled this remarkable work with powerful scriptures and personal wisdom, all of it so timely and practical. After living long with pain and quadriplegia, I know firsthand the enormous impact prayer has on one's ability to persevere through heart-wrenching suffering — so get out your prayer list, open the pages of Nancy's book, and pour the authority of Scripture over the wounds and weary hearts of those for whom you intercede! They will never be the same ... and neither will you."

Joni Eareckson Tada, founder, Joni and Friends International Disability Center

"This is a beautiful Scripture-grounded and Jesus-centered guide for praying for those who are hurting. Nancy Guthrie is gold and so is this book!"

Randy Alcorn, author; founder and director, Eternal Perspective Ministries

"This unique book is a precious gift for God's people. In these short, devotional chapters, Nancy Guthrie teaches us to pray more effectively — more specifically and more biblically — for those around us who are going through trials and suffering. Unlike any book on prayer that I've ever seen, this is not a book that you simply *read* ... this is a book that you use. And I will use it often!"

Scott Anderson, President & CEO, Desiring God

"This book is a brilliant idea. It will help many of us pray for, and encourage, our brothers and sisters who are suffering. I thank God for it."

Christopher Ash, Writer-in-Residence, Tyndale House, Cambridge

"The prayers of God's people have always been a precious and priceless gift to me, but never more than during my husband's recent journey with cancer. This wonderful, practical resource from Nancy Guthrie will help you give the gift of encouragement by praying biblically-grounded prayers for friends who are going through the fire and by sharing how you are praying for them that day."

Nancy DeMoss Wolgemuth, author, *Revive Our Hearts* founder, and Bible teacher

"In *I'm Praying for You*, Guthrie has written the most practical, scripture-infused guide to prayer that I have ever seen. When someone near us is suffering in some way, we often spontaneously say we'll pray for them. Often we don't follow through or if we do, we don't know how to pray. In forty short devotionals, each guided by the comfort and call of the gospel, Guthrie teaches us what it looks like to pray for someone with clarity and confidence, knowing that what we are praying is consistent with what God so graciously has revealed to us in his Word about who he is, what he has done and is doing for us and the life he has called us to as his children. As you walk with people through the troubles of life in this fallen world, you will turn to this little gem of a book again and again."

Paul David Tripp, pastor, event speaker, and author of many books including *New Morning Mercies*.

I'm Praying for You

40 Days of Praying the Bible for
Someone Who is Suffering

I'm praying for you

NANCY GUTHRIE

Unless otherwise stated, Scripture quotations are from the *Holy Bible*, New Living Translation, copyright © 1996, 2004, 2015 by Tyndale House Foundation. Used by permission of Tyndale House Publishers, Inc., Carol Stream, Illinois 60188. All rights reserved.

Scripture quotations marked ESV are from The Holy Bible, English Standard Version. ESV® Text Edition: 2016. Copyright © 2001 by Crossway Bibles, a publishing ministry of Good News Publishers.

British Library Cataloguing in Publication Data
A record for this book is available from the British Library

ISBN: 978-1-913896-25-6

Designed by Jude May
Cover image © KatyaKatya | Adobe Stock

Printed in Denmark by Nørhaven

10Publishing, a division of 10ofthose.com
Unit C, Tomlinson Road, Leyland, PR25 2DY, England
Email: info@10ofthose.com
Website: www.10ofthose.com

Contents

7

QR Code Instructions

Throughout this book we've included QR codes that will enable you to easily load and send a message to those you are praying for, letting them know exactly how you are praying for them on that day. You can practice using the test code below.

On iPhone:
1. Open the camera app on your phone.
2. Point your phone and focus on the QR code — this should scan it.
3. A pop-up window will appear. Now, press and hold until two options appear: 'Search Web' or 'Copy'.
4. Click 'Copy' then go to your preferred messaging app and press and hold to paste the text there.
5. Send the message to your friend to let them know that you are praying.

On Android:
1. Some android phones include a built-in QR scanner. You can test this by pointing your camera at the QR code on this page, or by using Google Lens.
2. If this doesn't work, go to the app store and download a QR Reader — there are many free options.
3. Open the app, point your phone and focus on the QR code — this should scan it.
4. Select text, click 'Copy', then go to your preferred messaging app and press and hold to paste the text there.
5. Send the message to your friend to let them know that you are praying.

I'm praying John 9:3 for you today, praying that you will sense that your suffering is not meaningless, but purposeful. I'm praying that people around you will see that God is at work in your life so that his glory will be on display for the world to see.

Introduction

When someone we care about is going through something difficult, we are quick to say, "I'm praying for you!" But then what? Do we really pray? And if so, what do we pray? How do we know what to pray?

If we're honest, most of us might have to admit that we have a rather limited vocabulary when it comes to praying for others who are suffering. Our prayers are often limited only to asking/begging God to take away the suffering. Certainly, this is a good instinct! We pray, asking God to work, because we believe that he is able and inclined to do good toward those he loves. But our prayers tend to be mostly guided by what we think would be the best outcome for the situation, or for what the person who is suffering has asked us to pray.

If we really believe that God is sovereign over our suffering (and why would we even consider praying if we didn't?), and that he is purposeful in allowing suffering into the lives of those who belong to him, shouldn't that shape how we pray? Shouldn't we welcome God to accomplish everything he intends to accomplish uniquely through the suffering for that person's good and for his glory?

The Bible helps us to do that. The Bible provides us with a vocabulary for prayer that enables us to ask God to achieve what he intends in and through the suffering in our lives and the lives of those we care about. So, let's use the words the Bible provides to call upon God. Rather than presume upon him to accomplish his good purposes in the life of the person who is suffering, let's plead with him to do it! In the pages that follow, we'll work our way through forty Scripture passages that reveal something about God's purposes in suffering. The Scriptures aid us in offering prayers that God delights to answer. They help us to ask him rather than presume upon him to do what he has promised to do. And they keep us from becoming too focused on demanding that he do what he has not promised to do.

We'll consider carefully what God is saying in those verses and then we'll turn the words of that passage into a prayer. You'll be able to insert the name of the person you're praying for into the provided prayer. Using the QR code at the end of each prayer, you'll also be able to load and send a personal text message to the person you're praying for so that he or she will know not only *that* you are praying, but exactly *what* you are praying. In this way, each day's Scripture passage will not only guide your prayer, it will also focus and encourage the person for whom you're praying. We're going to pray for healing, relief, and restoration. But we won't stop there because the Bible doesn't let us stop there. Instead of praying only for the brokenness to be made whole, we're going to pray that the glory of God's character would be on display uniquely through the broken places. We're going to approach prayer not as a tool to manipulate God to get what we want, but as a way to submit to what he wants. Through prayer, we will draw close to him in our need. We'll welcome him to have his way because we believe that he is good and that his plans for us, and all who are his, are good.

There may be some prayers in this book that seem insufficient because they petition God to work in and through your friend's suffering rather than remove the suffering. Perhaps these prayers won't always seem bold enough or big enough. But when we allow the Bible to shape our prayers, we can actually be sure that our prayers are right-sized and rightly focused. Perhaps they will seem, at times, too focused on anticipating the joys of the life to come rather than petitioning God to deliver those joys in this life. Much of modern Christianity has taught us to pray this way. But the consistent focus of the Scriptures is a call to set our hope on the life to come in the presence of God, which will commence on the day of resurrection. The Scriptures encourage eager longing for that day.

My hope is that this little book will help you to do what I know you really want to do, which is to faithfully pray for the person you care about who is in need of prayer. Out of a desire to keep sentences as uncomplicated and unencumbered as possible, and to make reading and praying with this book as personal as possible, I've used a variety of pronouns throughout. You'll find that I go back and forth between referring to the person being prayed for as a him or a her. I hope you'll make the needed adjustment as you read and pray.

So, let's begin. Let's pray. Let's allow the Bible to give shape and substance to our prayers. Let's pray in full confidence that God himself is giving us the inclination to pray, the words to pray, and the comfort of knowing that the Spirit is interceding with groanings that go beyond what we pray. Let's pray in confidence that God delights in our prayers and hears our prayers. Let's pray to our Father who invites us to bring all of our needs and concerns to him today, and looks forward to us coming back to ask him for his help again tomorrow.

1

I'm praying that the work of God will be displayed in your life

"It was not because of his sins or his parents' sins," Jesus answered.
"This happened so the power of God could be seen in him."

John 9:3

Jesus had just healed a man who had been blind since birth. And the disciples had a question. It's the same question we all have when we suffer: Why? But their question included an assumption. They asked, "Why was this man born blind? Was it because of his own sins or his parents' sins?" (John 9:2). Did you catch the assumption in their question? They assumed that the man's suffering was caused by someone's sin. They just didn't know whose.

The disciples' question was completely focused on the *cause* of the man's suffering. Notice, however, that Jesus' answer to their question "Why?" was all about *purpose*, not *cause*. It's as if he wanted to turn their gaze from the past to the present and the future. It's as if he wanted to get them less focused on pointing the finger of blame and more focused on

15

seeing the way he was putting his glory on display. They were all caught up in what *caused* the blindness but Jesus pointed them toward the *purpose* God had in it. The purpose, according to Jesus, was that the power of God, the work of God, the glory of God would be put on display in this man's life. In fact, this is a purpose God has in every believer's life.

So, let's pray that the work of God will be put on display in the life of the person for whom we're praying. Perhaps the work of God will be put on display in the way it was in this man's life — in the form of supernatural healing. Or perhaps it will be put on display in some other way as his Holy Spirit goes to work in the interior of our friend's life, transforming his or her character, perspective, interactions, opinions, and desires.

We all know that people observe those who are suffering to see if Jesus makes any difference at all when the worst things happen. Let's pray that they will see that Jesus is really making a difference in the way our friend suffers — that the work of God will be put on display for all who are watching.

. . . .

Prayer

Lord, we don't presume to know exactly what your purpose is in allowing this suffering into _____'s life. But we believe that because he belongs to you, his suffering is not random or meaningless. It's purposeful. And so we ask you to accomplish your purposes. We ask that your power at work in _____'s life would be seen in his life. May all he comes in contact with see that your Spirit is at work generating the fruit that only he can produce—the fruit of love, joy, peace, patience, kindness, gentleness, and self-control. Lord, work a miracle in _____'s life. Work in such a way that it is obvious to all that something supernatural is taking place in his body and in his soul.

. . . .

I'm praying John 9:3 for you today, praying that you will sense that your suffering is not meaningless, but purposeful. I'm praying that people around you will see that God is at work in your life so that his glory will be on display for the world to see.

2

I'm praying that the Lord will take away your pain

So to keep me from becoming proud, I was given a thorn in my flesh, a messenger from Satan to torment me and keep me from becoming proud. Three different times I begged the Lord to take it away. Each time he said, "My grace is all you need. My power works best in weakness."

2 Corinthians 12:7–9

Whenever we suffer, it is natural to ask, "Why?" But when Paul was given a thorn in the flesh (whatever it was) that brought him unrelenting agony, interestingly he didn't ask, "Why?" He seemed to know exactly *why* God had allowed this pain into his already pain-ridden life. He looked at the thorn and he saw the hand of God at work in his life, protecting him from sin. Paul had been granted the kind of spiritual experience that could make a person's head swell with spiritual pride — the opportunity to see into the glories of heaven. So, in the pain of the thorn, Paul saw God at work protecting him from something that would be even more painful—allowing this supernatural experience to fill him with spiritual pride.

But while Paul saw the hand of God at work in the thorn, he saw another hand at work as well. He recognized it as a "messenger from Satan" to torment him. Paul was tormented with the temptation to resent God for allowing the thorn to invade his already pain-ridden life. What God intended to develop his faith, Satan wanted to use to diminish his faith. What God intended to use to train Paul to trust him, Satan wanted to use to tempt Paul to resent him.

So, Paul knew that God was at work for his good through the thorn … and he still begged God to take it away. And then he begged again. And then he begged again. Most of us can relate to that. Even when we can see that God is using the hurts in our lives to accomplish something good in us, we still want the pain to stop.

Paul actually heard Jesus speaking to him in response to his begging for the thorn to be taken away. But it can't have been what he was hoping to hear. Jesus' answer to Paul's repeated prayer was not that he would take the thorn away, but that he would provide Paul with enough grace to endure living with the thorn. Paul would experience divine power, not in the thorn being removed, but in its being redeemed.

. . . .

Prayer
Lord, it is such a relief to know that you are sovereign over the pain in _____'s life. Give _____ the firm confidence that what Satan may intend to use to diminish her faith, you will use to develop her faith. We beg you to take away this pain. And we know you can. But if you choose not to, give _____ the grace and power to endure the pain.

. . . .

I'm praying 2 Corinthians 12:7–9 for you today, begging God to take away your pain. How I pray he will bring you relief! But I'm also thanking him for the grace he has promised to provide so that you can endure the pain that he does not take away.

3

I'm praying that this trial will develop your endurance

Because of our faith, Christ has brought us into this place of undeserved privilege where we now stand, and we confidently and joyfully look forward to sharing God's glory. We can rejoice, too, when we run into problems and trials, for we know that they help us develop endurance. And endurance develops strength of character, and character strengthens our confident hope of salvation. And this hope will not lead to disappointment. For we know how dearly God loves us, because he has given us the Holy Spirit to fill our hearts with his love.

Romans 5:2–5

The Bible continually sets before us a future to lean into and look forward to: a future in which we will share in the radiant, holy, satisfying, joyful glory of God. But sometimes in the midst of suffering in this life, that future can seem so far away with so many difficult days in between.

In Romans 5, Paul seems to want us to think and feel differently about the problems and trials that plague us as we await eternal glory. He seems to want us to recognize that the problems and trials of this life are actually productive in our lives, helping us to set our hope more fully on what he has prepared for us. Instead of being frustrated or resentful about the suffering in our lives, Paul says that we can be genuinely happy. This joy is caused by recognizing that every day, as we experience God providing what we need to endure faithfully, something is being developed in us: a patience with trials; a rugged joy in disappointment; and a firm confidence that the God who supplied what we needed to get through today will provide what we need tomorrow too.

And as we endure faithfully, we realize something else is happening. A strength of character is developing in our lives so that we are less fussy, less entitled, less self-centered. We recognize that the Holy Spirit really is at work transforming us from the inside. The genuineness of our faith strengthens our confidence that God really has saved us, is saving us, and will one day save us from this sin-sick world to live in his presence. We become more convinced that we will never regret putting all of our hope in Christ.

. . . .

Prayer

Lord, as _____ deals with the difficulties this day brings, help _____ to remember that you are at work in the midst of problems and trials to develop something in _____. Do your work developing perseverance so that _____ will be able to trust and love you over the long haul. Do your work of developing Christ-like character in _____ so that _____ will radiate the beauty of Christ for all to see. Fill _____ with confidence that he will never regret putting all of his hope in you and what you are preparing for those who love you.

. . . .

24

I'm praying Romans 5:1–5 for you today, asking God to develop in you everything that he intends in the midst of the problems and trials today brings. I'm asking him to give you what you need to keep going and to fill you with confidence that you will never regret putting all of your hope in him.

4

I'm praying that the Lord will keep you

The LORD spoke to Moses, saying, "Speak to Aaron and his sons, saying,
Thus you shall bless the people of Israel: you shall say to them,
The LORD bless you and keep you;
the LORD make his face to shine upon you and be gracious to you;
the LORD lift up his countenance upon you and give you peace."

Numbers 6:22–26 (ESV)

Sometimes when we suffer, it seems as if God has turned against us, as if he is withholding his goodness from us. But these words of blessing that God told Moses to pronounce over his people as they wandered in the wilderness should convince us otherwise. They reveal God's settled disposition toward his people, his posture toward those he calls his own. He intends to bless us and keep us, to be gracious to us, to give us peace.

God took the initiative to assure his people of his settled intention to bless them. He wanted to make it clear that he intended to be personally involved in their lives as the source of all the goodness they would enjoy.

Isn't it good to know that the Lord's settled disposition toward you and the person you are praying for is that of blessing?

But what does it mean to be blessed? Certainly, as we live in this world that has been impacted by the curse, we would not identify so many of our experiences as "blessings." Yet experiencing God's blessing is not merely getting what *we* deem to be good things *from* God. The essence of blessing is getting more *of* God.

When we ask God to bless the person we're praying for, we're asking God to make him deeply content in God. We're praying that he finds his home so securely in God that adverse circumstances cannot shake him. We're praying that he will sense God's smile on his life. The face of God is radiant toward those who are his because he sees us not for who we are on our own, but for who we are in Christ. He is not focused on what we've done, good or bad, but on what Christ has done on our behalf. To ask God to bless the person we're praying for is to pray that he will live each day in peace knowing that God is not stingy with his grace and goodness. God's settled intention is to show us his favor, or grace, when we turn to him. He will keep us safe in his care, even when our hearts are prone to wander.

. . . .

Prayer

Lord, you are the source of all true blessing and we know that you love to bless your people. So, we ask you to be true to your word. Bless _____ with the goodness of your felt presence; keep _____ secure in your love; give _____ a tangible sense of your smile on his life; extend grace to _____; turn your gaze toward _____ in mercy; and give _____ the kind of peace that only comes from you.

. . . .

I'm praying Numbers 6:22–26 for you today, asking the Lord to be true to his promised intention to bless you and keep you. I'm asking him to make his presence known to you, to be full of grace toward you, and to give you supernatural peace. I'm praying you will have the grace to live this day like you are blessed—because you are.

5

I'm praying that you will not fear bad news

Praise the Lord!
How joyful are those who fear the Lord
and delight in obeying his commands ...
They do not fear bad news;
they confidently trust the Lord to care for them.

Psalm 112:1, 7

When we have repeatedly received bad news — from the doctor, from the accountant, from the counselor, from family members — we find ourselves always bracing for more bad news. Anticipating the next blow can become a way of life.

We don't want the person we're praying for to adopt this way of life. Instead, we pray that she will experience the joy that is described in Psalm 112. This psalm presents an idyllic picture of the lives of those who put their hope in the gospel and thereby receive the righteousness of Christ by faith. Obeying the Lord delights them. Having confidence in God to take care of them seems to make them impervious to living in constant fear. They are not always waiting for the other shoe to drop, for something terrible to happen. Such a person, according to this psalm, does not live in fear of bad news.

We want the person we're praying for to have the blessedness of confident trust that the Lord is committed to caring for her. We want her not to be always living on edge, but instead to be living at peace, confident that being in God's hands is the safest place to be.

Psalm 112 helps us to see that the answer to our ongoing anxieties is not a hoped-for turn of events, but rather a God-centered stance of trust. He is a God who loves to bless his people. When we know this deep in our souls, instead of living in fear of bad news, we live in the confident expectation that he is at work for our good and for his glory.

. . . .

Prayer
Lord, replace any fear of bad news in _____'s heart and mind with fear of you, confidence in you, hope in you. Fill _____ with the joy that comes from fearing you and the delight that comes in obeying you. May the anxieties about the problems _____ is facing today and _____'s fears about the future give way to confident trust that you are at work.

. . . .

I'm praying Psalm 112 for you today, praising the Lord for the joy he gives to those who fear him so that they don't have to fear bad news. I'm asking him to give you that joy.

6

I'm praying that God will make you strong and immovable

So, my dear brothers and sisters, be strong and immovable. Always work enthusiastically for the Lord, for you know that nothing you do for the Lord is ever useless.

1 Corinthians 15:58

The essence of our Christian hope is centered not on having our best life now, and not merely on going to heaven when we die. Rather, what the Bible puts forward again and again for us to hope in is the promise of resurrection. In fact, Paul says that "if Christ has not been raised ... your faith is useless ... And if there is no resurrection of the dead, then Christ has not been raised ... And if our hope in Christ is only for this life, we are more to be pitied than anyone in the world" (1 Corinthians 15:14, 16, 19).

But a future day of resurrection, when Christ will return to this earth and call our bodies out of the grave to be reunited with our souls, can

35

seem so ethereal, so distant. We wonder if nurturing our hope in a future day of resurrection can really make any difference in how we face the difficulties of life now. At the end of this chapter on resurrection, Paul points to the difference a solid confidence in resurrection should make in the lives of believers. It should make us strong and steadfast. Confidence in the coming resurrection keeps us going until our work is done. It makes us immovable, meaning that we don't easily lose our balance and get knocked down. We have our minds firmly planted in God's word so that crazy ideas don't find any foothold in our thinking. As the winds blow through our lives in the form of difficulty, sickness, financial pressure, relational strife, or loss, we do not veer off course. We remain clear and resolute on what is true, what is reliable, and what is forever. We remain convinced that the gospel is true, and that Christ has ultimate authority over everything — even death.

The promise of resurrection keeps us from insisting that this life provide us with everything we long for. It reorients our gaze toward the resurrection life to come, making us strong and immovable in loving the Lord, relishing his promises, singing his praise, and living like we really do believe that day is coming.

. . . .

Prayer

Lord, may the truth of the resurrection of Jesus and the certainty of the resurrection of all believers make _____ strong and steadfast. May it make _____ immovable, looking to you as his only hope.

. . . .

36

I'm praying 1 Corinthians 15 for you today, asking God to so work the hope of resurrection in you that you will be strong and unmovable in your affection and allegiance to him. I pray that you'll serve him gladly, believing that your love and obedience will matter into eternity.

7

I'm praying you will find fellowship with Jesus as you share in his sufferings

I want to know Christ and experience the mighty power that raised him from the dead. I want to suffer with him, sharing in his death, so that one way or another I will experience the resurrection from the dead!
Philippians 3:10–11

In the midst of suffering, we find ourselves looking for someone "safe" to whom we can draw close. We're most comfortable with someone who has been there, someone who has suffered in the way that we are suffering, someone who has tasted pain rather than remained aloof from it.

In the midst of suffering, we discover that Jesus is actually a safe person to draw close. He gets it. He understands. Matthew records that as he went into the Garden of Gethsemane, he said to Peter, James, and John, "My soul is crushed with grief to the point of death" (Matthew 26:38 and Mark 14:34). Jesus understands what it is like to feel as if sorrow is pressing the life out of you. He understands the sick feeling in your stomach, the heaviness on your chest, the lump in your throat. Jesus felt the pressure of grief so much that he had a physical reaction to it. Sweat was dripping off him as he poured out his prayers to the Father, asking that the cup of suffering be taken away from him. Jesus knows what it is like to pray desperate prayers that God would save him from suffering. And he knows too the experience of having God, by his seeming silence and lack of intervention, say "no" to his request.

Most of us would say that we want to be close to Jesus. But we don't want to have to suffer to experience that closeness. Yet how do we think we could draw close to a suffering Savior if we never experience suffering ourselves?

. . . .

Prayer
Lord, would you draw _____ close to you in suffering? Would you give _____ a sweet taste of what it means to fellowship with you in your suffering? Would you fill _____ with a sense of companionship with one who understands overwhelming sorrow, a dread of pain, and prayers answered differently from how she hoped.

. . . .

I'm praying Philippians 3:10–11 for you today, asking that you would experience sweet fellowship with Jesus as you share in his sufferings, and that it will fill you with assurance that you will also share in his resurrection!

8

I'm praying that God will make you fruitful

I am the true grapevine, and my Father is the gardener. He cuts off every branch of mine that doesn't produce fruit, and he prunes the branches that do bear fruit so they will produce even more.

John 15:1–2

God is the Master Gardener. He is, even now, tending his garden, nurturing it toward a great harvest. And according to this verse, his work of gardening includes a lot of cutting. He cuts off every branch that doesn't produce fruit. In other words, those who are not truly joined to him in a life-giving way, those whose lives demonstrate that they are spiritually dead, can anticipate being cut away from his life-giving presence.

But notice that there is also cutting in the lives of those who are spiritually alive. God is at work cutting away anything and everything that will keep us from growing, keep us from producing the fruit of his Spirit, keep us from becoming all that he intends for us to be. This pruning often looks like a cutting away of things in our lives that we enjoy and value. This cutting usually hurts. It doesn't seem fair. It doesn't seem right. But the cutting isn't intended to hurt us. It is intended to prune us toward greater fruitfulness. The cutting is what is necessary for our ultimate flourishing, our greater growth.

When a plant has been cut back, it can look bare for a while. It can seem as if the gardener has been completely ruthless, that perhaps he's overdone it. But then the seasons change and there is new growth in different directions, new beauty in a different shape, blossoming life in what seemed to have been damaged.

Here is the truth for each one of us: God, the Master Gardener, is going to do some cutting in our lives. He's either going to cut us away, or he's going to prune us for greater fruitfulness. Let's pray that his pruning in our lives, and those we are praying for, will produce the fruit he intends.

. . . .

Prayer
Father, as we see your pruning work in _____'s life, it can sometimes seem that you're being cruel. The cutting away is painful. Please help _____ to trust that you are the Master Gardener. You know just where to cut, when to cut, and how much. Give _____ eyes to see that you are purposeful in the pruning and that you intend for his life to produce beautiful fruit that will please him and please you. Keep _____securely connected to Jesus, the true vine.

. . . .

44

I'm praying John 15:1–2 for you today, asking God to keep you securely connected to Jesus, the true vine, even as the pruning he is doing in your life is painful. I'm asking him to take great care in the cutting so that your life will bear bountiful fruit for him.

9

I'm praying that God will cause everything to work together for your good

And we know that God causes everything to work together for the good of those who love God and are called according to his purpose for them. For God knew his people in advance, and he chose them to become like his Son, so that his Son would be the firstborn among many brothers and sisters.

Romans 8:28–29

No one likes to have Romans 8:28 quoted at them. It makes us feel like people are telling us we should be happy about the things in our lives that are clearly not good — because God is going to bring some good out of it. It seems to send some people on a search to find something good that has happened as a direct result of the bad thing, and to evaluate whether or not that goodness is worth the suffering involved. But all of us are profoundly grateful that Romans 8:28 is in the Bible. It means that if we are in Christ, we can be sure that our suffering is not random or meaningless. It's purposeful. And oh, how we want the suffering in our lives to have meaning and purpose.

Perhaps the hardest word to swallow in Romans 8:28 is "everything." It means that there is nothing that falls outside of this promise. In his sovereignty, God is committed and able to use even the worst things we can imagine for our ultimate good.

And we don't have to go on a search to figure out what that "good thing" is. Paul tells us in the next verse. The good purpose he has in the hardships and catastrophes and hurts in our lives is this: that we would become like his Son, Jesus. God's good purpose is to work together everything that we experience, encounter, and endure to create in us a family resemblance and family relationship with his Son, Jesus.

Embracing and welcoming God to accomplish this purpose in our lives requires that we let go of our desires for a comfortable life. But it enables us to embrace a life of purpose and meaning even when that includes pain.

. . . .

Prayer

Lord, either everything works for our good, or nothing makes sense. Give _____ a deep and undergirding confidence that you can and will cause everything to work together for good because _____ belongs to you. Use this suffering we would not describe as good for _____'s good. Use it to shape _____ into the image of your Son, Jesus.

. . . .

48

I'm praying Romans 8:28–29 for you today, asking God, in his sovereignty, to cause all things in your life — even and especially the hard and bad things — to work together for your good. May he accomplish his good purpose of conforming you more closely to the image of his Son, Jesus.

10

I'm praying for you to be healthy in body and strong in spirit

The elder to the beloved Gaius, whom I love in truth. Beloved, I pray that all may go well with you and that you may be in good health, as it goes well with your soul. For I rejoiced greatly when the brothers came and testified to your truth, as indeed you are walking in the truth. I have no greater joy than to hear that my children are walking in the truth.

3 John 1–4 (ESV)

In the brief letter of 3 John, we get to read a personal letter between the apostle John and a man named Gaius, one of John's beloved spiritual children. John had received a report from someone who had recently been with Gaius that Gaius was strong in spirit. In this letter to his friend, John told Gaius how happy it made him to receive such a good report about the state of Gaius's soul and the integrity of Gaius's life as he lived out the truth of the gospel. John also told Gaius how he was praying for him: that his physical health would be as strong as his reported spiritual health.

It is helpful to see here that John's love for his dear friend Gaius led him to pray for Gaius's physical health. We are body and soul, and to love someone is to have concern for, and therefore pray for, health in body and soul. But sometimes we may get this a bit out of balance. We're comfortable checking in with each other in regard to health issues. It comes naturally to us to ask and offer prayers regarding physical health concerns. But we don't always do as well when it comes to checking in with each other in regard to spiritual health. That can seem too personal. We don't want to put the other person on the spot. Few of us are willing to raise our hand when prayer requests are being taken to ask for prayer because we're struggling with doubt, or discouragement, or fear, or prayerlessness, or a resistance to believing and obeying God. We'd much rather stick with asking for prayer for physical and perhaps more superficial things.

But as we seek to be a faithful friend to someone who is suffering, we want to pray for health in both body and soul. This means we may need to ask what can seem to be a profoundly personal question as we inquire about the state of their soul. We might say, "I'm praying for a number of your physical health concerns. How can I pray for your spiritual health?"

. . . .

Prayer

Lord, I thank you that your love and care for us extends to both body and soul. Our bodies are so vulnerable to sickness in this world, and our souls are too. I ask you to give _____ physical vigor and health as only you, the Healer, can provide. I also pray that you will give _____ insight into areas of spiritual sickness that need your healing touch. Heal _____ in body and soul for your glory and gladness.

. . . .

I'm praying 3 John 1–4 for you today, asking God to give you health in body and soul. May you experience the strength of spirit that comes from living out the truth of the gospel.

11

I'm praying that you will not worry about your life

Can all your worries add a single moment to your life? And if worry can't accomplish a little thing like that, what's the use of worrying over bigger things? ... These things dominate the thoughts of unbelievers all over the world, but your Father already knows your needs. Seek the Kingdom of God above all else, and he will give you everything you need.
Luke 12:25–26, 30–31

When Jesus asked these penetrating questions of his disciples, it was because they were filled with anxiety about having enough — enough food to eat; enough clothes to wear. Of course, we too are disciples who are filled with anxiety about whether or not we will have enough — enough energy to keep dealing with the difficult issues; enough insight to see the problems clearly as well as come up with workable solutions; enough money to pay the bills; enough time to do what needs to be done.

Jesus asks if worry has the creative power to actually add to our lives. And as soon as we hear the question, we know the answer. We know that all of the energy we give to worry is really only robbing us of peace. None of us have the ability to add a single hour to our lives, or the lives of those we are praying for through worry.

We do have something that should make all the difference when we are tempted to worry — we have a Father who knows our needs and will provide everything we need. So, instead of marinating in our fears about the future, we can turn every worry that enters into our mind into prayer and thereby begin to experience a restful confidence in God.

. . . .

Prayer
Father, worry comes so naturally. Help _____ to turn every worry that begins to generate anxiety into a prayer. Keep _____ from lying awake at night rehearsing worries. Give _____ restful confidence throughout the day and throughout the night in a loving Father who knows what is needed and is committed to providing it.

. . . .

I'm praying Luke 12:25–31 for you today, asking the Father to keep you from worry and give you a restful confidence that he knows your needs and will provide everything you need.

12

I'm praying that you will consider this trial as an opportunity for joy

Dear brothers and sisters, when troubles of any kind come your way, consider it an opportunity for great joy. For you know that when your faith is tested, your endurance has a chance to grow. So let it grow, for when your endurance is fully developed, you will be perfect and complete, needing nothing.

James 1:2–4

It hits us as completely counter-intuitive that when troubles come our way, we should consider them opportunities for great joy. We more naturally think of them as opportunities to complain, to doubt, to indulge in self-pity, or simply to make the best of a bad situation until it resolves. But James says that we should "consider it" differently. In other words, we should think about troubles differently — in a way that will cause us to feel differently.

We can have great joy in the midst of troubles as we consider what our faithful endurance in those trials is accomplishing or generating in the interior of our lives. Something is being developed in us that simply can't be developed through ease or comfort or increasing Bible knowledge. God intends to use the troubles at hand to develop in us a deeper, stronger, and more mature dependance on him. And that has the power to fill us with joy.

Our troubles are giving us an opportunity to live out the faith we claim. As our faith is put to the test through trials, we are called upon to persevere — to keep choosing to trust and rest and find our comfort in God alone. And as we persevere, we find we are "growing up" in our faith. Our roots are going down deeper into God. Joy comes as we contemplate emerging from the suffering as people who have a stability and steadfastness that makes us less easily shaken by difficult circumstances in the future.

. . . .

Prayer

Lord, would you give _____ the ability to think about trouble very differently than most people do. Help _____ to consider it as an opportunity for great joy. As _____'s faith is tested, cause endurance to grow and develop, making _____ perfect and complete, needing nothing.

. . . .

I'm praying James 1:2–4 for you today, asking God to help you to consider the troubles in your life as an opportunity for joy. I know that sounds strange. But I'm praying that you'll have the joy that comes from believing and sensing that this trial is developing your endurance and making you into the mature believer he intends for you to be.

13

I'm praying that God will give you a "but even if he doesn't" faith

Shadrach, Meshach, and Abednego replied, "O Nebuchadnezzar, we do not need to defend ourselves before you. If we are thrown into the blazing furnace, the God whom we serve is able to save us. He will rescue us from your power, Your Majesty. But even if he doesn't, we want to make it clear to you, Your Majesty, that we will never serve your gods or worship the gold statue you have set up."

Daniel 3:16–18

It must have been an incredible scene. Thousands of people from throughout the kingdom of Babylon gathered to dedicate the ninety-foot golden image that Nebuchadnezzar had set up. As instructed, they were bowing down to the statue. But in the sea of people with faces to the ground, three men remained standing, knowing full well a fire was being stoked for all who refused to bow. They were called before King Nebuchadnezzar, who said to the three young men, "I will give you one more chance to bow down and worship the statue I have made when you hear the sound of the musical instruments. But if you refuse, you will be thrown immediately into the blazing furnace. And then what god will be able to rescue you from my power?" (Daniel 3:15).

Shadrach, Meshach, and Abednego knew that their God was able to rescue them. What they didn't know was whether or not that rescue was part of his divine plan. What was it that enabled Shadrach, Meshach, and Abednego to face the fire not knowing if God would rescue them? God's promise of ultimate rescue into a kingdom that will last forever and their certainty in ultimate resurrection.

At the end of the book of Daniel, we read that the archangel Michael pointed Daniel to a day in the future when "every one of your people whose name is written in the book will be rescued. Many of those whose bodies lie dead and buried will rise up, some to everlasting life and some to shame and everlasting disgrace. Those who are wise will shine as bright as the sky, and those who lead many to righteousness will shine like the stars forever" (Daniel 12:1–3). It is confidence in this future reality that filled them with courage and still fills believers with courage to face the fires of life.

. . . .

Prayer

Lord, we know that you are able to rescue, able to heal, able to protect and provide, able to miraculously work. But we don't know if that is how you intend to be glorified in this circumstance. Please give _____ the kind of faith that will enable _____ to trust you even if you do not rescue in the way we have in mind. Give _____ the courage to put full confidence in your ultimate rescue on the day of resurrection.

. . . .

I'm praying Daniel 3:16–18 for you today, asking God to give you such a solid confidence in the security of his kingdom and the certainty of his ultimate rescue from death that you'll be able to face the uncertainty of his rescue in your current circumstances.

14

I'm praying that God will give you the grace to wait

O LORD, don't rebuke me in your anger
or discipline me in your rage.
Have compassion on me, LORD, for I am weak.
Heal me, LORD, for my bones are in agony.
I am sick at heart.
How long, O LORD, until you restore me?
Return, O LORD, and rescue me.
Save me because of your unfailing love.

Psalm 6:1–4

It can be so very hard to wait on God to heal and restore. We pray earnestly for three or four days, and we think of ourselves as having persevered in prayer. Of course, when we've prayed for months or years and see no tangible evidence of God at work in response to our faithful prayers, we can begin to lose hope. We wonder if heaven is closed to us or if there really is anyone in heaven who is listening and able to act.

We can relate to David's cry of "How long, O Lord ... ?" He gives us words to express our own frustration with what can sometimes seem like slowness on God's part. But his words also remind us to whom we're praying. David was praying to the God of unfailing love. That's what kept David praying for what seemed to him to be much too long. He knew that it is God's essential nature to be merciful, and that he was praying to a God who hears, who answers, who rescues. So, he kept praying.

When we are sick at heart, troubled in body and soul, wondering if God is even hearing our prayers, we can be sure that he has heard. When we are worn out from sobbing, we can be sure that the Lord has heard our weeping. He has heard our pleas and will answer. It may not be today or tomorrow. In fact, God may not accomplish all the healing and restoration we long for in the person we are praying for in this lifetime. But we can be sure that the day will come when his work in our lives and the lives of those we love will be brought to completion. He will return. He will rescue. He will save because of his unfailing love.

. . . .

Prayer

Lord, sometimes it seems that you work so slowly. Give _____ the patience to wait for you to accomplish all you intend. Even when _____ can't see that you are working, give _____ the faith to believe that you are, in fact, working in the waiting. Even when it seems as if it's taking too long, give _____ the faith to trust you to accomplish all you intend to accomplish right on time.

. . . .

I'm praying Psalm 6 for you today, which gives us words to express how hard it is to wait for God to do his work of healing and restoration. I'm praying that God will give you the grace to wait on him and to keep on asking him to heal you in body and soul.

15

I'm praying for you to be able to focus on running toward the heavenly prize

I press on to possess that perfection for which Christ Jesus first possessed me. No, dear brothers and sisters, I have not achieved it, but I focus on this one thing: Forgetting the past and looking forward to what lies ahead, I press on to reach the end of the race and receive the heavenly prize for which God, through Christ Jesus, is calling us.

Philippians 3:12–14

In the midst of hardship, it can be easy to become obsessed with our pain, unable to think or talk about anything else. We easily become focused on doing whatever it takes to get to the good life in the here and now. But in Paul's letter to the believers in Philippi, we see that Paul maintained a very different focus in the midst of his suffering in prison.

Paul saw this life in Christ as a race that has a finish line. And he was focused on finishing his race well. He wanted to continue to invest everything he could in advancing the kingdom of God. He refused to allow the suffering of prison to lull him into complacency or comfort-seeking or self-centeredness. Rather than focusing on being cold, forgotten, treated harshly, and unjustly accused, Paul was focused on the ultimate goal of life in Christ: to reach the end of the race and receive the heavenly prize, the Father's "well done." He was focused on living all out for Christ in this life, believing that it would result in reward and gladness in the life to come.

Paul's example in focusing on this one thing — what lies ahead for us in heaven — challenges us to evaluate our own focus in the midst of suffering. Focusing on what is to come fills our ordinary days with eternal purpose. We stop trying to force all that awaits us in the new creation into the here and now, and instead, "press on to possess that perfection for which Christ Jesus first possessed" us.

• •

Prayer

Lord, we hear you calling us to press on in this race, which is leading us toward a heavenly life with you. Forgive us for being so shortsighted to expect that we can experience all of heaven's joys and perfections in the here and now. Fill _____ with the energy needed to keep pressing on today and tomorrow and for all the days to come. Fill _____ with greater anticipation of what is to come, making apprehension of the heavenly prize the focus of _____'s thoughts, words, and actions.

• •

I'm praying Philippians 3:12–14 for you today, asking God, by his Spirit, to give you the energy and clear focus you need to press on toward the heavenly reward awaiting you at the end of your race.

16

I'm praying for you to live in a way that pleases the Lord

So we have not stopped praying for you since we first heard about you. We ask God to give you complete knowledge of his will and to give you spiritual wisdom and understanding. Then the way you live will always honor and please the Lord, and your lives will produce every kind of good fruit. All the while, you will grow as you learn to know God better and better. We also pray that you will be strengthened with all his glorious power so you will have all the endurance and patience you need. May you be filled with joy, always thanking the Father. He has enabled you to share in the inheritance that belongs to his people, who live in the light.

Colossians 1:9–12

It is good to ask the person we're praying for if there is anything in particular they want us to pray about. Of course, oftentimes they have a very specific end toward which they want us to pray. They have determined what they think would be the best outcome to the crisis they are facing and so they ask us to petition God to work toward that preferred outcome.

But is our human estimation of what would be best a reliable end to pray toward? And if not, how do we know what might be a reliable end to pray toward? Paul points us toward the best possible end in his prayer for the believers in Colossi. He says that ever since he heard about them, he has not stopped praying for them. There is something that needs to develop in their lives that is so important, he is constantly praying about it. It is the same thing that needs to develop in our lives and the life of the person for whom we are praying.

Paul seems to understand something about human nature. We are inclined to pursue what pleases us. It comes naturally to organize our lives and commitments around pleasing ourselves. But what keeps Paul on his knees in prayer for the Colossian Christians is that they would have the spiritual wisdom and understanding to live toward a different end. He prays that they would orient their lives in the pursuit of honoring and pleasing the Lord. He wants them to know God's will, but not merely as an intellectual accomplishment. He's praying that as they steadily grow in their understanding of what the Scriptures reveal as pleasing to God, they will persist in conforming their lives to it, and that the result will be that God will be honored and pleased.

. . . .

Prayer
Lord, I pray now and will never stop praying for _____ because _____ will always need knowledge of your will and the spiritual wisdom and understanding to live it out. Give _____ the desire to live in a way that will always honor and please you. Work in _____ to produce every kind of good fruit.

. . . .

I'm praying Colossians 1:9–12 for you today, asking God to give you complete knowledge of his will. I'm asking him to give you the kind of spiritual wisdom and understanding that will enable you to orient your life toward pleasing and honoring him.

17

I'm praying that there will be a harvest of righteousness in your life

For our earthly fathers disciplined us for a few years, doing the best they knew how. But God's discipline is always good for us, so that we might share in his holiness. No discipline is enjoyable while it is happening — it's painful! But afterward there will be a peaceful harvest of right living for those who are trained in this way.

Hebrews 12:10–11

There's a big difference between punishment and discipline. Punishment is intended to be punitive, to make the person pay for wrong. All who are in Christ need never fear that their suffering is a result of being punished for sin. How do we know that? Because Christ has already been punished for our sin, so we don't have to be.

But discipline is different. Discipline is purposeful. Discipline is something a loving father does. The writer of Hebrews tells us, "the LORD disciplines those he loves" and, "No discipline is enjoyable while it

79

is happening — it's painful" (Hebrews 12:6, 11). "... endure this divine discipline," the writer encourages. "God's discipline is always good for us" (Hebrews 12:7, 10). God is the perfect parent. His discipline is never too harsh or inappropriate. We do not always know how best to discipline our children, but God does. He always knows and does what is right.

Obviously, experiencing discipline doesn't feel good at the time. It feels like hardship and loss and pain. But we can endure his discipline in our lives because while it's painful, we're confident it's purposeful. God's purpose in disciplining us is that we might "share in his holiness." God wants his children to bear the family resemblance. He wants us to live in a way that demonstrates that we share the passions and priorities of our Father. When we are willing to be trained by his discipline — to be molded and shaped by it — something beautiful happens. Something blossoms in our lives — a peaceful harvest of right living.

. . . .

Prayer
Heavenly Father, we never grow beyond our need for your loving discipline. So, keep loving _____ by disciplining _____ in the way that only you can. But please, be gentle. Give _____ the grace to endure your divine discipline and give _____ the joy of experiencing a peaceful harvest of right living as _____ increasingly shares in your holiness.

. . . .

80

I'm praying Hebrews 12 for you today, asking your heavenly Father to be gentle with you as he works in and through the suffering in your life to discipline you toward increasingly sharing in his holiness.

18

I'm praying that God will give you the faith to trust him

Some trust in chariots and some in horses,
but we trust in the name of the LORD our God.

Psalm 20:7 (ESV)

It would have been perfectly natural for the king of Israel to put his trust in the size and capabilities of his standing army. That's what kings did in his day. But David wasn't like other kings. He knew he was a vice-regent to a greater king who was the real source of security for his people. So, rather than trust in military might, David was determined to trust in God alone. He proclaimed, "Now I know that the LORD rescues his anointed king. He will answer him from his holy heaven and rescue him by his great power" (Psalm 20:6).

Similarly, it is perfectly natural for us to put our trust in many things that seem to offer security. We put our trust in good healthcare and good habits. We find security in savings accounts and insurance policies.

We put our trust in our own powers of persuasion or personal grit.

But at the heart of what it means to follow God is making him the center and source of our security. We don't want to put our confidence in worldly safeguards and solutions. We know our future does not depend on the protection, opportunities, or income we can provide for ourselves. We trust in the name of the Lord our God. At least we want to do so.

We need the Lord's help to put our trust in him to provide, instead of trusting in savings accounts and insurance policies. We need his help to trust him to protect, instead of trusting in health regimens and safety precautions. We need his help to trust that he has preordained every day of our lives, instead of trusting in our own plans and dreams. We need his help to trust in what Christ has accomplished on our behalf, instead of trusting in what we can achieve. So, we pray, asking him for the faith to trust him with everything.

. . . .

Prayer

Lord, it is so natural to trust in what we can see and touch rather than in a God we can't see. So, give _____ eyes of faith to see how worthy you are of trust. You are the only true and lasting security in this uncertain world. Help _____, Lord, when _____ is tempted to put hope and confidence in what may seem certain, but is ultimately unstable. Keep calling _____ to trust you with everything.

. . . .

84

I'm praying Psalm 20:7 for you today, asking God to give you the faith you need to trust in him for everything. I pray that you will refuse to trust in anything or anyone else in this world for the ultimate security and salvation only God can provide.

19

I'm praying that you will remain faithful

As for me, my life has already been poured out as an offering to God. The time of my death is near. I have fought the good fight, I have finished the race, and I have remained faithful. And now the prize awaits me — the crown of righteousness, which the Lord, the righteous Judge, will give me on the day of his return. And the prize is not just for me but for all who eagerly look forward to his appearing.

2 Timothy 4:6–8

Our modern culture tends to deny the reality that death comes to each one of us, and often sooner than we expect. Some even see it as morbid to think soberly about such things. But we don't find that in the Bible. The Bible encourages us to live in light of the reality of death.

In the closing words of Paul's letter to Timothy, his son in the faith, Paul writes a farewell that we might hope to be able to emulate. His accomplishment is what we might hope to be able to claim as our own when our lives draw to a close. Paul had written long before to the

Philippians, "I long to go and be with Christ, which would be far better for me" (1:23). Now his longing was about to be fulfilled. But there was no fear in death for Paul. He had been pouring out his life as an offering, as a living sacrifice, for thirty years. He was at peace as he faced death because he didn't see his death as the end.

Paul fought the good fight against discouragement, unbelief, and self-pity. He didn't give up when things got hard. He kept a firm grip on the faith. He kept on taking Christ at his word, kept on relying on Christ's finished work, and kept on guarding the gospel.

It can be hard to imagine a day when our days will be complete, and we will be preparing to leave this life for the next. But that day is coming for each one of us. Oh, that we would be able to echo these words of Paul, that our lives would evidence the same fight, the same endurance, the same rugged faith.

• •

Prayer
Lord, we don't know if _____'s death is near or far out in the future. But we do know that unless you return first, that day will come. Fill _____ with the will to keep fighting the fight of faith, to keep running the race, to remain faithful. Set _____'s heart even now on the day when _____ will receive the prize, having eagerly looked forward to your appearing.

• •

I'm praying 2 Timothy 4:6–8 for you today, asking God to provide what you need to keep up the fight of faith, to keep running the race of faith, to remain full of faith in Christ and his promised reward. I'm asking him to increase your eagerness for his return.

20

I'm praying that you will rely on God and not yourself

We think you ought to know, dear brothers and sisters, about the trouble we went through in the province of Asia. We were crushed and overwhelmed beyond our ability to endure, and we thought we would never live through it. In fact, we expected to die. But as a result, we stopped relying on ourselves and learned to rely only on God, who raises the dead.

2 Corinthians 1:8–9

Even if we are smart enough to know that "God helps those who help themselves" isn't in the Bible, we still sometimes live as if this is gospel truth. Most of us don't enjoy being needy or having to depend on others. We want to come up with and carry out our own solutions to our problems. We want to be strong and capable and recognized for overcoming difficulties. We tend toward assuming that self-reliance is something God values as much as we do. But evidently, he doesn't. As our heavenly Father, God actually works in overwhelming circumstances to cause us to rely fully on him rather than ourselves.

In his letter to the Corinthians, Paul described a time when he and his ministry companions were in a situation so dire that they thought they were going to die. Whatever it was, and whatever caused it in human terms, Paul saw that God was at work for his good. God was using those circumstances to rid Paul and his companions of any lingering tendency toward self-salvation. Evidently, they were in a situation in which they couldn't rely on their own creativity, abilities, efforts, or resourcefulness. Their only source of salvation was God. And evidently it was good for them to come to the realization that God was their only hope. God used this hardship to teach Paul to rely more fully on him.

In this same way, God uses the situations in which we come to the end of our rope and the end of our own resources to draw us toward himself, to remind us that he values dependance, not independence.

. . . .

Prayer

Lord, there are days when _____ feels crushed and overwhelmed beyond the ability to endure. Help _____ to see this trouble as an opportunity to learn to rely more fully on you. You are the God who raises the dead, which means that you have the power to bring life from death. Show your power in _____'s life in the way you see fit.

. . . .

I'm praying 2 Corinthians 1:8–9 for you today, asking that when you feel overwhelmed beyond your ability to keep going, you'll experience what it means to rely more fully on God rather than yourself.

21

I'm praying that you will love and forgive others the way God has loved and forgiven you

Since God chose you to be the holy people he loves, you must clothe yourselves with tenderhearted mercy, kindness, humility, gentleness, and patience. Make allowance for each other's faults, and forgive anyone who offends you. Remember, the Lord forgave you, so you must forgive others. Above all, clothe yourselves with love, which binds us all together in perfect harmony. And let the peace that comes from Christ rule in your hearts. For as members of one body you are called to live in peace. And always be thankful.

Colossians 3:12–15

When a part of our body is bruised or burned, we're much more sensitive to pressure being put on it. When something or someone rubs up against it, we react. Similarly, when we are experiencing physical, emotional, and relational pain, we're more sensitive, more likely to react when something or someone rubs us the wrong way. Our quick and sometimes harsh responses can be hurtful to those around us and damaging to our witness and our relationships. This is when we are more desperate than ever for qualities of Christ to overflow into our lives and onto those around us.

As recipients of tenderhearted mercy, kindness, gentleness, and patience from God, we want to extend tenderhearted mercy, kindness, gentleness, and patience in our words and demeanor to those around us. We want our reactions and relationships to be marked with a sense of harmony and peace that comes from Christ ruling in our hearts. As those who have been shown such abundant grace by our heavenly Father, we want to extend grace to those who hurt or disappoint us. We want to make allowance for the faults of others and forgive them when they offend us. We want to resist keeping a record of wrongs. We refuse to insist that we be the primary recipient of care and concern, and orient ourselves toward caring for the needs of others. As those who have been dearly loved by our heavenly Father, we want to clothe ourselves in his way of loving.

. . . .

Prayer
Lord, would you cause the tenderhearted mercy, kindness, humility, gentleness, and patience you have shown to _____ to overflow to those around _____. Help _____ to recognize what is worthy of confrontation and correction, and what should be lovingly overlooked. May the peace that comes from Christ rule in _____'s heart.

. . . .

96

I'm praying Colossians 3:12–15 for you today, asking God to allow the flood of mercy, kindness, gentleness, and patience that he has shown to you to overflow through you toward those who hurt or offend you with their words or actions. I'm asking that his peace would rule in your heart today and every day.

22

I'm praying that you will not give in to discouragement

Why am I discouraged?
Why is my heart so sad?
I will put my hope in God!
I will praise him again—
my Savior and my God!

Psalm 42:5–6

Deep discouragement is not easily overcome. We need divine help. And that is what we're given in Psalm 42.

In Psalm 42, the psalmist finds himself homesick for God, longing to feel close to him again, asking, "When can I go and stand before him?" (Psalm 42:2). The difficulties of his life seem to mock his dependence on God: "Day and night I have only tears for food, while my enemies continually taunt me, saying, 'Where is this God of yours?'" (Psalm 42:3). He begins to remember how things used to be when he felt close to God and was able to sing for joy with real conviction. As he compares how it used to be with how it is now, his heart breaks.

But then it is as if something startles him out of his trajectory toward despair. He starts to question his own feelings and assumptions. Rather than accept and become defined by his very real and desperate feelings, he begins to interrogate them. He asks himself why he is so discouraged and sad. Rather than only listening to himself, he begins to preach the truth about who God is to himself. He chooses to call to mind the way the Lord daily pours out his love on him, the way the Lord is there to hear his prayers in the night.

David shows us what it looks like and sounds like to fight discouragement. He speaks to his own soul, telling himself to put his hope in God rather than give in to despair. And we can do the same thing as we make the words of Psalm 42 our own, reminding ourselves to hope in God rather than give in to discouragement.

. . . .

Prayer

Thank you, Lord, for giving us words in this psalm, not just to speak to you or to say things about you, but words to preach to ourselves in the midst of grief and discouragement. I pray that when _____ is deeply discouraged and can't see the way forward—when emotions are whispering that there is no reason to expect any good in the future—that you will give _____ the will to say, "I will put my hope in God!" Fill _____ with tangible hope that will diffuse the discouragement.

. . . .

I'm praying Psalm 42 for you today, asking God to dispel any discouragement with genuine hope. I'm praying that you will not simply listen to your own desperate thoughts but will talk back to them, reminding yourself to hope in God.

23

I'm praying that thinking about the inheritance being kept in heaven for you will make you smile

All praise to God, the Father of our Lord Jesus Christ. It is by his great mercy that we have been born again, because God raised Jesus Christ from the dead. Now we live with great expectation, and we have a priceless inheritance—an inheritance that is kept in heaven for you, pure and undefiled, beyond the reach of change and decay. And through your faith, God is protecting you by his power until you receive this salvation, which is ready to be revealed on the last day for all to see.

1 Peter 1:3–5

As much as we might seek to save and invest, conserve and protect, all of our possessions and wealth in this world are vulnerable — vulnerable to misuse, mismanagement, deterioration, unstable markets, or theft.

This vulnerability can generate a lot of fear. It can leave us grasping for security as we face an uncertain future.

This is when we need to meditate on the ultimate source of our security. Our security isn't in anything we create or accumulate in the here and now. It is being kept not in a vault or account on earth, but in heaven, the place of ultimate security and wealth, the place of incredible joy and satisfaction. When we enter into the new heaven and new earth and take possession of the inheritance that is being prepared and protected for us, we will not be disappointed. We'll be full of joy to receive all that God has for us and all that he will be to us.

But God does more than protect our inheritance in heaven. He also protects us until we receive this inheritance: "God is protecting you by his power until you receive this salvation," Peter writes. What good news it is that our salvation does not depend on our ability to hold on to Christ, but on Christ's ability to hold on to us!

. . . .

Prayer
By faith in your word I see your outstretched hands, Lord.
In one hand you hold an unfathomable inheritance, and
in the other you hold _____. Both are safe with you.
Please fill _____ with a restful sense of security today.
Fill _____ with joy now over all that will be _____'s
to enjoy forever.

. . . .

I'm praying 1 Peter 1:3–5 for you today, asking God to give you a restful sense of your security in him. I'm praying that it will make you smile as you think about all you stand to gain in his presence when you leave this life for the next.

24

I'm praying that you will sense the Holy Spirit praying for you

And the Holy Spirit helps us in our weakness. For example, we don't know what God wants us to pray for. But the Holy Spirit prays for us with groanings that cannot be expressed in words. And the Father who knows all hearts knows what the Spirit is saying, for the Spirit pleads for us believers in harmony with God's own will.

Romans 8:26–27

Sometimes, in the midst of difficulties, we say, "I guess all I can do is pray." But when things go not just from bad to worse, but from agonizing to unbearable, we sometimes find ourselves unable to form any meaningful prayers. We can't think clearly enough to connect the promises of God to our experience. And God seems far away.

It is then, when we have come to the end of ourselves, that we enter into a deep mystery. When we are reduced to helplessness, the Holy

Spirit helps us. When we can't string together the words to offer a coherent prayer, the Holy Spirit prays for us, not with words, but with groanings that cannot be expressed in words. When the familiar words and phrases seem hollow and rote, we can depend on the Holy Spirit to pray on our behalf. The Spirit prays profound prayers, passionate prayers, perfect prayers.

When we are weak — undone, confused, in anguish, can't think straight, overwhelmed with anxiety — how good it is to know that the Spirit not only indwells us; he helps us. He lightens our load. He comes alongside to engage with us in this work of prayer.

. . . .

Prayer

Father, we don't know what to pray for. We don't know what your will is. We don't always have the right words. So, thank you for the Holy Spirit who prays for _____ with groanings that cannot be expressed in words.

. . . .

I'm praying Romans 8:26–27 for you today, thanking God for the Holy Spirit who indwells you, for his readiness to help you, and for his groaning in prayer for you when you don't have the words to pray yourself.

25

I'm praying for you to bring honor to the name of Jesus

So we keep on praying for you, asking our God to enable you to live a life worthy of his call. May he give you the power to accomplish all the good things your faith prompts you to do. Then the name of our Lord Jesus will be honored because of the way you live, and you will be honored along with him. This is all made possible because of the grace of our God and Lord, Jesus Christ.

2 Thessalonians 1:11–12

We learn in the first part of Paul's second letter to the believers in Thessalonica that they were afflicted and suffering. So, how did Paul pray for those he cared about who were suffering? Paul's prayers for others were never general or generic, never selfish or shortsighted, never for external or temporal matters. As we listen in on Paul praying for those he loved, we discover he has something to teach us about how we ought to pray for those we love.

Paul asked God to enable the believers in Thessalonica to live in such a way that they would deserve the name they bore — the name of Christ. In other words, he didn't want them to live in hypocrisy, calling themselves Christians while living in a way that was anything but Christlike. He asked God to give them the spiritual power they needed to do the things the Bible instructed them to do — such as exercise their spiritual gifts, endure under persecution, and provide for the needs of the poor among them. As they lived, gave, and loved in these ways, Paul's greatest desire would be accomplished — that "the name of [the] Lord Jesus will be honored."

As we follow Paul's example in praying for those who are suffering, we pray that they will have the power to accomplish all the good things their faith prompts them to do — that even when they are short on patience, they will interact with others in a way that honors Christ; that even when they want everything to be all about them, they will be concerned for others; that even when they have very real questions about what God is doing, they will rest in confidence that what he is doing is good.

. . . .

Prayer

Lord, may your grace at work in _____ make it possible for _____ to live a life worthy of your call. Give _____ the power to accomplish all the good things faith prompts him to do. May the name of the Lord Jesus be honored because of the way _____ lives, and may _____ experience the joy and privilege of being honored along with Jesus.

. . . .

112

I'm praying 2 Thessalonians 1:11–12 for you today, asking God to give you the grace to live a life that is worthy of him and the power to accomplish all of the good things faith prompts you to do. May the name of Jesus be honored by the way you live.

26

I'm praying for the power of Christ to rest on you

But he said to me, "My grace is sufficient for you, for my power is made perfect in weakness." Therefore I will boast all the more gladly of my weaknesses, so that the power of Christ may rest upon me. For the sake of Christ, then, I am content with weaknesses, insults, hardships, persecutions, and calamities. For when I am weak, then I am strong.
2 Corinthians 12:9–10 (ESV)

When Jesus said to Paul, "My grace is sufficient for you," he was telling Paul — and he is telling you and me when we repeatedly pray for relief from the pain in our lives that does not come — *I will be enough for you in this. I will strengthen you for this. You can be confident that my grace will be delivered to you in the form and quantity and timing in which you need it. I will give you the grace you need to endure the pain I am not going to take away.*

This is incredible! It's more than we would ever think to ask for! The grace God provides is enough to generate joy in the midst of great sorrow. It's enough to endure criticism and obstacles everywhere you turn. It's enough to enable you to continue believing God is good and that he loves you even when he has withheld what you have so desperately sought from him.

Jesus also said to Paul, "my power is made perfect in weakness." Because of this, Paul became determined to boast gladly in his weaknesses "so that the power of Christ" would rest on him. Just think about this power, "the power of Christ." This is the power that enabled Jesus to endure the cross, the power that enabled him to forgive those who spat on him and hurled insults at him and betrayed him. This is the power that comes to rest on those who are joined to him by faith. His power comes to rest on us and radiate through us.

Christianity is often reduced to a method to make life go well. But spiritual strength is not about having such a special connection to God that we are able to convince him to say "yes" to our requests to change our circumstances. The supernatural experience God has promised is this: the power of Christ coming down to rest on us when the worst thing we can imagine happens to us or to someone we love.

. . . .

Prayer

Lord, may your promise of sufficient grace settle deep into _____'s soul. May the power of Christ come down to rest on _____ in such a way that _____ will have the strength to be content even if circumstances don't change. In _____'s weakness, show yourself to be strong.

. . . .

I'm praying 2 Corinthians 12:9–10 for you today, asking God to supply you with his promised sufficient grace that will enable you to endure faithfully. I'm asking that the power of Christ will rest on you, giving you the strength to be content in your challenging circumstances.

27

I'm praying for you to trust the Lord for your security

Those who trust in the LORD are as secure as Mount Zion;
they will not be defeated but will endure forever.
Just as the mountains surround Jerusalem,
so the LORD surrounds his people, both now and forever.

Psalm 125:1–2

"Those who trust in the LORD." We immediately want to put ourselves in that category, especially if there was a particular time when we made a commitment to trust him with our lives. Trusting the Lord is the foundation of faith and relationship with Christ, but it can be so very difficult to live consistently in this way — especially when we have to trust him with something precious to us such as our children or our livelihood, or with the possibility of disability or death.

Psalm 125 speaks some sense to us when we are tempted to put our trust in anything other than God. It tells us that our lives are as secure as

Mount Zion. In other words, our lives are as likely to crumble, as likely to be destroyed, as Mount Zion is likely to come down. Not only do our lives have the stability of Mount Zion, they also have the protection of the one who made the mountains. Our protection is his personal project; it is not assigned to lesser beings. Jehovah himself encircles his people. His protection is not occasional or temporary; it is now and for all time.

Trusting God means connecting ourselves to the one person who will endure forever. We simply can't provide this kind of security for ourselves or those we love. So, we trust in the Lord to be our security and protection.

. . . .

Prayer

Lord, we want to do more than just give lip service to trusting you. We want to deeply, consistently, pervasively entrust our lives and everything about them to you. Surround _____ even now with your protection. Protect _____ from discouragement. Protect _____ from resentment. Fill _____ with a sense of the security that comes from having you as our God.

. . . .

I'm praying Psalm 125 for you today, praising God for the complete security that is yours because you trust in him. I'm asking him to surround you and protect you from discouragement, alienation, and resentment.

28

I'm praying that the genuineness of your faith will result in glory to Jesus

In this you rejoice, though now for a little while, if necessary, you have been grieved by various trials, so that the tested genuineness of your faith — more precious than gold that perishes though it is tested by fire — may be found to result in praise and glory and honor at the revelation of Jesus Christ.

1 Peter 1:6–7 (ESV)

Peter writes that we can have joy even when we seem to have troubles coming at us from every direction. What is the source of that joy? According to Peter, we can have joy now because of something that will happen long after our suffering is over — on the day that Jesus returns. We can have joy now as we anticipate what will happen then as a direct result of the way we respond to our present difficulties.

On that day, the genuineness of our faith — as revealed by the way we continued to love and trust and live for Christ in the hardest of times

— will result not simply in reward for us, but also in greater praise and glory and honor being given to Jesus.

We can't really imagine how this will happen or what this will be like. But we can believe it is true and allow this future reality to fill us with counter-intuitive joy in the present. One reason we know this kind of joy is possible is that Jesus had this joy as he faced the worst suffering of all time. We read in Hebrews that it was the joy set before him that enabled Jesus to endure the cross and its shame. Because Jesus is the author and perfecter of our faith, we can expect that he can and will give us the same kind of faith and joy. No wonder Jesus will receive praise and glory and honor on that day!

There is a sense in which this promise forces us to think deeply about what we want most out of this life, about the purpose for which we're living. Are we living and praying toward shortsighted ends? Or are we living and praying for the end for which God made the world and has called a people to himself? Does the anticipation of glory given to Jesus in the future give us joy now?

. . . .

Prayer
Lord, would you fill _____'s imagination with the vision of a day in the future when you will receive great praise and glory and honor as a result of the faith you have given to _____? Would you fill _____ with anticipatory joy now in that future day?

. . . .

I'm praying 1 Peter 1:6–7 for you today, asking God to fill you with anticipatory joy as you think about the day when Jesus returns and receives praise, glory, and honor because of the genuineness of your faith in him in the midst of challenging circumstances.

29

I'm praying you'll be able to say to your Father, "I want your will to be done, not mine"

My Father! If it is possible, let this cup of suffering be taken away from me. Yet I want your will to be done, not mine.

Matthew 26:39

As we come to the Father, pouring out our righteous, repeated, vigorous prayers, it helps us to observe and overhear what happened when Jesus did that very same thing. When we read the gospel accounts of Jesus praying in the Garden of Gethsemane, we find him unashamedly pouring out what he wanted to his Father. He desired there to be some other way of satisfying the justice of God besides offering himself as a sacrifice for sin. If there was any other way, he did not want to have to experience the separation from his Father that becoming sin would demand. So, three times Jesus pleaded for his Father to let the cup of suffering be taken away from him.

There is no record of a response from God. But clearly, in the corresponding silence, Jesus heard God saying "no" to his request.

Overhearing Jesus' prayer and God's answer helps us in at least two ways. First, it frees us to pour out what we want before God. We are free to pour out our honest desires to our Father. But it also shows us what it looks like to express, along with our wants, our deeper desire for whatever God wants. When we truly believe that God's plans for us are even better than we could plan for ourselves, we are able to tell him that we want what he desires more than we want to get our own way.

The second way overhearing this prayer and God's answer helps us is as we realize that if God said "no" to the prayer of Jesus, his Son—who was perfectly obedient, who prayed in complete accordance with the will of God—then his saying "no" to us is not because we were not obedient enough or spiritual enough or didn't pray hard enough, long enough, or passionately enough. We tend to think it is these things that unlock the door to God's "yes." So, when we see that God said "no" to Jesus, we begin to realize that prayer is not primarily about getting a "yes" from God, but rather about relationship with our Father. It's about bringing our will into submission to our Father's will.

• •

Prayer

Father, if it is possible, please let this cup of suffering be taken away from _____. But if your good and wise plan includes no relief, no rescue, please give _____ such confidence in you that _____ can welcome your will to be done. Give _____ the grace to say along with Jesus, "I want your will to be done, not mine" and really mean it.

• •

I'm praying Matthew 26:39 for you today, thanking God for the example of Jesus in freely pouring out his wants to his Father as well as his example of submission to his Father's will.

30

I'm praying you will know the Lord is watching over you

I look up to the mountains—
does my help come from there?
My help comes from the LORD,
who made heaven and earth!
He will not let you stumble;
the one who watches over you will not slumber.
Indeed, he who watches over Israel
never slumbers or sleeps.

Psalm 121:1–4

As the people of God made their way from the plains in Judea up the hill to Jerusalem for various feasts and festivals, they sang the Songs of Ascent together. At times they must have looked ahead to the heights they had to climb and wondered how they would have the strength for them. And when they did, Psalm 121 provided words for them to ask and answer that question out loud together. Singing together on their way upward, they declared together that the Lord they were on their way to meet at the Temple would be their help. He could see the unseen pitfalls ahead and wouldn't let them stumble. He would never cease his careful watching over them.

As Psalm 121 must have been for them, it can be for us a meditation on God's around-the-clock watching over our lives. The psalm is a way to remind ourselves that nothing can happen outside his direction. "No one can snatch [us] from the Father's hand" (John 10:29).

Sometimes the road of suffering can seem like a very steep hill. We wonder if we will have the strength to keep putting one foot in front of the other over the long haul. When we're tired and afraid, we can remind ourselves that the one who called us to himself and started us on this journey toward the New Jerusalem in his presence will help us all along the way. He knows the potential pitfalls and places where we could go wrong, and he will keep us on the right path. He will never be asleep at the wheel when it comes to sovereignly overseeing our lives. He will never become bored with or uncaring about the concerns we pour out in prayer.

. . . .

Prayer

Lord, I pray you will give _____ increased confidence in your promised help for whatever _____ must deal with today and tomorrow and the day after that. Keep _____ from stumbling and falling away from you. Keep watch over _____ in the details of the day and the anxieties of the night. Watch over _____'s coming and going both now and forever.

. . . .

I'm praying through Psalm 121 for you today, asking God to give you confidence in his promised help, his protection, and his watchful care over you.

31

I'm praying that God will give you an eternal perspective on your pain

In his kindness God called you to share in his eternal glory by means of Christ Jesus. So after you have suffered a little while, he will restore, support, and strengthen you, and he will place you on a firm foundation. All power to him forever! Amen.

1 Peter 5:10–11

Peter clearly had a timeline in his mind as he wrote his letter to suffering believers scattered throughout Asia. He declared that they were being guarded through faith for a salvation "ready to be revealed *in the last time.* In all this you greatly rejoice, though now *for a little while* you may have had to suffer grief in all kinds of trials" (1 Peter 1:5–6 NIV, my italics). He called them to set their hope fully on the grace that will be brought to them "when Jesus Christ is revealed" (1 Peter 1:7). "The end of all things is at hand," he wrote in 1 Peter 4:7 (ESV).

Then near the end of his letter, he wrote, "after you have suffered *a little while*" (my italics). Was his encouragement to the believers of his day that they should anticipate that their time of suffering in this life would be limited in duration? Perhaps more significantly for us, can we read this and assume that though we may suffer, it shouldn't last very long?

When Peter wrote that we may suffer "a little while," he was looking at the suffering of this life from the perspective of eternity. The only way to describe the suffering that has come and not gone, with no apparent end in sight, as lasting "a little while" is if we compare the timeline of our lives to the endless line marked "eternity." The reality of what Peter is saying to believers in his day and to us is this: *Your suffering might last for the rest of your life, but in light of the never-ending glory you are going to share with Jesus, it is really only a little while.*

What enables us to endure a lifetime of suffering is knowing that we will share in Jesus' *eternal* glory. In eternity, a lifetime of physical, emotional, or relational pain will seem like it only lasted a little while.

. . . .

Prayer
Lord, in your kindness, you called _____ to share in your eternal glory by means of Christ Jesus. Please give _____ a tangible sense of that eternal glory. Fill _____ with restful confidence that after suffering a little while, you will restore, support, and strengthen _____. You will place _____ on a firm foundation. All power to you forever! Amen.

. . . .

I'm praying 1 Peter 5:10–11 for you today, asking God to give you such a tangible sense of how long eternity will be and how great the glory is that he intends to share with you. I pray that reality will shape your perspective regarding the trials of this life that seem to last so long.

32

I'm praying for you to grasp how deeply you are loved by God

I fall to my knees and pray to the Father, the Creator of everything in heaven and on earth. I pray that from his glorious, unlimited resources he will empower you with inner strength through his Spirit. Then Christ will make his home in your hearts as you trust in him. Your roots will grow down into God's love and keep you strong. And may you have the power to understand, as all God's people should, how wide, how long, how high, and how deep his love is. May you experience the love of Christ, though it is too great to understand fully. Then you will be made complete with all the fullness of life and power that comes from God.

Ephesians 3:14–19

One of the first things that is called into question when we suffer significantly is the love of God. We think, "God, if you really loved me, you wouldn't allow this; you would fix this." Our tendency is to look at the love of God through the lens of our circumstances. Instead, we need to look at our circumstances through the lens of God's love for us in Christ. The greatest demonstration of God's love for us happened when he gave his only Son to take our sin upon himself so that sin will no longer be a barrier between us and God. This incredible love is the lens through which we need to see his love for us.

What we need is a clearer and firmer grasp on the love of God, which is exactly what Paul prayed would be a reality in the lives of the believers in Ephesus. Paul wanted them to have Spirit-given strength in their inner being — specifically the strength to comprehend something that is otherwise incomprehensible. Paul knew that the Ephesian believers needed a clearer and firmer grasp on the expansive nature of God's love for them in Christ. He wanted their lives to be rooted and grounded in this love. He wanted them to believe, deep in their souls, that they were loved by God. As their roots went deep into the love of Christ, they would be able to withstand the winds of difficulty that would blow in their lives. They would have "the fullness of life and power" to persevere, which is generated by believing that we are loved by the Lord of the universe.

. . . .

Prayer

I fall to my knees and pray to you, Father, the Creator of everything in heaven and on earth. I pray that from your glorious, unlimited resources you will empower _____ with inner strength through your Spirit. May Christ make his home in _____'s heart as she trusts in him. May _____'s roots grow down into God's love and keep her strong. May _____ have the power to understand how wide, how long, how high, and how deep your love is. May she experience the love of Christ and be made complete with all the fullness of life and power that comes from you.

. . . .

140

I'm on my knees, praying Ephesians 3:14–19 for you today. I'm asking God to give you inner strength and the power to understand how expansive God's love is for you and how secure you are in it.

33

I'm praying that you will know God's presence with you in the darkness

O Lord, God of my salvation,
I cry out to you by day.
I come to you at night.
Now hear my prayer;
listen to my cry.
For my life is full of troubles,
and death draws near.
I am as good as dead,
like a strong man with no strength left.

Psalm 88:1–4

Psalm 88 is a song of Heman the Ezrahite. He writes, "my life is full of troubles, and death draws near." We don't know the nature of the suffering Heman the Ezrahite was going through, but we can relate to what he has written because of the honest way he describes his thoughts and feelings. He has no strength left. He feels forgotten and cut off from God's care. He perceives that God has thrown him into the lowest pit, the darkest depths, and left him there. He feels helpless, desperate, and alone. "Darkness is my closest friend," he declares (Psalm 88:18).

And then the psalm ends, with no tidy conclusion. Most laments in the psalms let in a ray of sunshine somewhere along the way or close with a confident note of determination to trust God. Not this psalm. There seems to be no resolution. But that does not mean there is no genuine hope. The light of redemption is faint in this psalm, but it's there. It is actually stated in the first verse, and evidenced by the psalm as a whole. Heman begins the psalm not by crying out to a powerless or uncaring God, but to the "God of my salvation." Underneath all of his despair is an undergirding confidence in God's salvation purposes in his life.

This psalm shows us that faith can be real even when there is no tidy conclusion, even when it cannot articulate strong hope, even when it's barely holding on, even when everything seems very dark. It helps us to keep coming to the Lord, even when it feels as if he does not hear and is refusing to act. As we do, we're reminded that the God of our salvation is the only one with the ability to pierce through the darkness of our difficult circumstances. He hears us when we cry out to him in the darkness because he is with us in the darkness.

· ·

Prayer
God of _____'s salvation, save _____ from despair. Save _____ from an inclination to run away from you rather than toward you with all of this pain. Save _____ from the voice that tells him that you have forgotten, that you are angry, that you have turned your face from him. Enter into _____'s darkness and illumine it with the light of your presence.

· ·

I'm praying through Psalm 88 for you today, asking the God of your salvation to save you from alienation from him, save you from despair, save you from giving up. I'm asking him to illumine the darkness in your life with the radiant light of his presence.

34

I'm praying that you will fix your gaze on things that cannot be seen

That is why we never give up. Though our bodies are dying, our spirits are being renewed every day. For our present troubles are small and won't last very long. Yet they produce for us a glory that vastly outweighs them and will last forever! So we don't look at the troubles we can see now; rather, we fix our gaze on things that cannot be seen. For the things we see now will soon be gone, but the things we cannot see will last forever.

2 Corinthians 4:16–18

Paul encourages us to do something in this passage that seems impossible. He calls us to "fix our gaze on things that cannot be seen." So, what are these invisible realities and how do we fix our gaze on them?

What can't be seen is the "glory that vastly outweighs" the heaviness of pain that life in this broken world brings. We're meant to fix our gaze on this glory. What comes naturally to us is to fix our gaze on our present troubles and to assume that they are random and meaningless. They certainly look that way on the surface. But Paul wants us to see that they are not meaningless or useless. They are producing something for us in a realm that we can't see with our physical eyes. Suffering for Christ and in Christ produces a weighty, eternal glory that we can't see now but will enjoy forever when we enter into his presence.

Fixing our gaze on this eternal glory does at least two things. First, it keeps us from giving up. It instills in us a rugged determination to look past our present pain toward the glory to come. Secondly, it gives us perspective. When Paul says, "our present troubles are small and won't last very long," we're tempted to think that he is diminishing the very real pain of life in this world. But he isn't. Our problem is one of perspective. We need the promises of Scripture to develop within us a holy imagination that will give us an ability to see the glory.

As we stop focusing on our troubles and fix our eyes on the glory to come, we find that it makes the heaviest burdens seem light. And as we consider just how long we will be enjoying that eternal glory, it has the power to make even lifelong struggles seem like they won't last very long.

. . . .

Prayer

Lord, keep _____ from focusing on present troubles which can loom so large and appear so relentless. Fix _____'s gaze on the realities that can't be seen with physical eyes, realities that put today's difficulties into eternal perspective.

. . . .

I'm praying 2 Corinthians 4:16–18 for you today, asking God to give you spiritual eyes to see the glory he intends to share with you into eternity. I'm asking him to make his promises regarding the glory to come loom so large in your thinking and feeling that today's troubles will seem small and insignificant.

35

I'm praying for God to work out his plans for your life

Though I am surrounded by troubles,
  you will protect me from the anger of my enemies.
You reach out your hand,
  and the power of your right hand saves me.
The LORD will work out his plans for my life—
  for your faithful love, O LORD, endures forever.
  Don't abandon me, for you made me.

Psalm 138:7–8

What kinds of things does God do with his hands? At creation he "laid the foundations of the earth, [his] right hand ... spread out the heavens above" (Isaiah 48:13). Moses told the nation of Israel that "the LORD your God brought you out [of Egypt] with his strong hand" (Deuteronomy 5:15), and after they were safely across the Red Sea, he sang, "Your right hand, O LORD, smashes the enemy" (Exodus 15:6). A short time later, after the people of Israel walked across the dried-up Jordan River, Joshua told them that the Lord had done it "so all the nations of the earth might know that the LORD's hand is powerful, and so you might fear the LORD your God forever" (Joshua 4:24).

Amazingly God, in a sense, "gets his hands dirty" as he works in the lives of his people to create, establish, rescue, protect, and lead them. Though he is transcendent, he is not distant or disengaged. He is actively at work in the lives of those whom he loves.

When he wrote Psalm 138, perhaps David was thinking of all these things God had done with his hands. As he thought about God using his hands to protect and preserve his people, it filled David with confidence that God would reach out his hands to save him and to work out his plans in his life. Of course, what David could not yet see clearly was the greatest work of protection and salvation the Lord's hands would provide — when God incarnate would give his hands over to evil men to have nails driven into them. Because of this work of his hands, we have every reason to expect that the Lord will not withhold anything good from us. He will surely work out all of his good plans for our lives.

. . . .

Prayer
Lord, remind _____ of your history of reaching out your hands to save your people. This is who you are and what you do. Even now, reach out your powerful right hand to save _____ from fear and alienation, from despair and discouragement, from resentment and regret. Protect _____ from the enemy of her soul. Continue working out your plans for _____'s life and give _____ the faith to believe those plans are good.

. . . .

I'm praying Psalm 138 for you today, asking God to use the power of his right hand to protect you, save you, and lead you into the good plans he has for your life. Rest in knowing that he will be faithful to you and will not abandon you.

36

I'm praying that you'll cast all your anxieties on God

Humble yourselves, therefore, under the mighty hand of God so that at the proper time he may exalt you, casting all your anxieties on him, because he cares for you.

1 Peter 5:6–7 (ESV)

None of us particularly relish the idea of being humbled. But Peter makes it clear that there is a particular kind of humbling that enables us to experience restfulness in the present and anticipate soul-satisfying exaltation in the future. This is not a humbling forced upon us, but rather a humbling we pursue in the midst of fears and worries and troubles.

This humbling begins as we admit that we simply cannot bear the weight of our concerns on our own. We don't have the inner strength to live with the inner turmoil. We don't have the power to change the circumstances. We don't know what needs to be done or how it will be accomplished. Rather than huddle under this load of concern and uncertainty and need, we actively cast the full weight of these things onto the only person who is both strong enough and caring enough to act and intervene.

We look up and see the mighty hand of God and we believe that his mighty hand is not over us to crush us but to care for us. We humble ourselves under God's mighty hand by putting all of our anxieties into his mighty hands. Through prayer, we name our fears and concerns one by one and cast them in God's direction. We pray to God like we really do believe that he is our burden-bearer and that he cares about what has our stomach in knots and our minds in turmoil.

Pride says, "If I don't figure this out, it won't get fixed." Pride says, "I've got to be strong. I can handle this." Humility says, "God, I need you to bear this burden, work in this situation, make a way for me. And I believe you will, because I'm convinced that you truly care for me."

. . . .

Prayer

Father, we are full of anxiety about things we have no power to control. We desperately need you to work, extending your mighty hand to deliver and redeem, to save and secure, to draw _____ to yourself. Give _____ the grace to cast every anxiety about the present and the future on you, knowing that you care and can be trusted.

. . . .

156

I'm praying 1 Peter 5:6–7 for you today, asking God to give you a sense of the safety to be found by humbling yourself under his mighty hand, and the rest to be found in casting all of your anxieties on him.

37

I'm praying that you will learn the secret of being content

Not that I was ever in need, for I have learned how to be content with whatever I have. I know how to live on almost nothing or with everything. I have learned the secret of living in every situation, whether it is with a full stomach or empty, with plenty or little. For I can do everything through Christ, who gives me strength.

Philippians 4:11–13

When we sing the hymn "It Is Well With My Soul," we sing, "Whatever my lot, thou hast taught me to say, it is well, it is well, with my soul." And when we sing these words, we so want this to be the reality of our own souls. So, how does it become so, or what teaches us to say and to experience this?

The apostle Paul wrote that he had "learned" to be content. His process of learning contentment included being inconvenienced, impoverished, mistreated, unfed, and uncomfortable. Certainly, he must have meditated on how Jesus was impoverished, mistreated, unfed, and uncomfortable. He must have found fellowship with Jesus uniquely as he shared in his sufferings. He must have meditated on all that was his because he was joined to Christ. Even though so much had been taken from him, Paul was able to see his lack in light of all he stood to gain. Paul's willingness to be content wasn't based on his expectation that his circumstances would change. He was determined to find his contentment in Christ regardless of his circumstances.

We think we'll be content when we finally get what we want, what we're praying for. But real contentment is when we accept less than or something other than what we want. Christ is our source for the spiritual strength we need to live with what we didn't ask for and less than we want.

. . . .

Prayer
Lord, as you have enrolled _____ in the school of suffering, teach the secret to being content, no matter what you provide or what you withhold. Give _____ what is needed to be content on the days when things are good and the days when everything feels hard. Fill _____ with the supernatural contentment that comes from being joined to Christ.

. . . .

I'm praying Philippians 4:11–13 for you today, praying that the strength that is yours because you are joined to Christ will enable you to be deeply and genuinely content in every situation that arises today.

38

I'm praying that you will wait with eager hope for Christ's return

Against its will, all creation was subjected to God's curse. But with eager hope, the creation looks forward to the day when it will join God's children in glorious freedom from death and decay. For we know that all creation has been groaning as in the pains of childbirth right up to the present time. And we believers also groan, even though we have the Holy Spirit within us as a foretaste of future glory, for we long for our bodies to be released from sin and suffering. We, too, wait with eager hope for the day when God will give us our full rights as his adopted children, including the new bodies he has promised us.

Romans 8:20–23

Anyone who thinks deeply about the suffering in his or her life eventually gets to the question, "Why?" We wonder, "Why me?" "Why this?" "Why now?" We often point to circumstantial reasons for the suffering, but in Romans 8, Paul helps us to see the most profound answer to our question,

"Why?" When we experience the impact of natural disasters and accidents, disease and death, it is because of what happened so long ago in the Garden of Eden. Sin entered into this world and corrupted everything. Because of the curse brought about by sin, nothing and no one escapes its impact.

But while Romans 8 encourages us to look backward into human history to find the cause of much of our suffering, it also points us toward the future, when the impact of the curse will be eradicated and everything will be made good again. This passage calls us to look up from our groaning over the impact the curse has had on the world and in our lives, and to look forward to something. It points us toward a day to long for more than we long for relief, more than we long for resolution. It points us toward the day when Christ returns, the day of resurrection.

It comes so naturally to set our hopes on much lesser things, but this passage provides us with needed perspective. We must see our short-term troubles in context of our long-term expectation. This frees us to groan, but it also keeps us from giving up. In the midst of our sorrow, the Holy Spirit generates increasing anticipation for the day when the new creation life that has begun in the interior of our lives will become the reality of all creation.

. . . .

Prayer
Lord, sometimes we groan as we wait for you to free the world from death and decay. The curse is so real, so present, and so pervasive. Even now _____ is feeling its effects. Thank you for beginning your work of bringing newness by creating new life in the soul of _____. I humbly ask you to extend that newness and restoration to _____'s body. I ask that you expand _____'s anticipation of the great resurrection day to come when all of creation will be made new.

. . . .

I'm praying Romans 8:20–23 for you today, asking God to meet you in your groaning and longing, and to fill you with perspective about what he has done and is doing to eradicate the curse that sin brought upon this world. I'm praying that he will give you a greater longing for the great resurrection day to come, when all of creation will be made new.

39

I'm praying that you will never forget the Lord's faithfulness to you in these days

I will never forget this awful time,
*   as I grieve over my loss.*
Yet I still dare to hope
*   when I remember this:*
The faithful love of the LORD never ends!
*   His mercies never cease.*
Great is his faithfulness;
*   his mercies begin afresh each morning.*
I say to myself, "The LORD is my inheritance;
therefore, I will hope in him!"

Lamentations 3:20–24

The Bible does not ignore the suffering of this life and how much it hurts. Instead, it gives voice to our suffering and gives us words to express to God himself how much life in this broken world can hurt. In the book of Lamentations, we find divinely inspired lament over unbearable suffering and lost hope. The very fact that it is included in the biblical canon assures us that God does not expect a stoic response from his people, as if the hurts inflicted on us have no effect, as if somehow we are immune from feeling loss deeply and desperately.

But the beauty of Lamentations is that it is not simply a venting of despair. Rather, the book of Lamentations provides us with perspective in the midst of despair. That's what seems to happen as the writer of Lamentations pours out his account of grief. It appears the mere mention of the divine name — the Lord of unfailing love — gets him thinking about the perfections of God that have become even more vivid to him uniquely because of the pain. God's faithful love never ends, his mercies never cease, his faithfulness will never fail. So, instead of continuing to listen to his despairing thoughts, the writer of Lamentations begins to talk back to himself. It's as if he says, *Self, everything you need, you have forever in Christ, so turn away from your despair and take hold of hope in God!*

It's good to know that our heavenly Father does not shush the laments of his children. But it is also good to know that he does not leave us hopeless in our laments. Instead, he beckons us to turn toward him with our sorrows and meets us with his faithful love and mercies.

. . . .

Prayer
Lord, when the sorrow of this life overwhelms _____, may _____ turn to you to pour out lament and gain perspective, rather than turn away from you and become bitter. Fill _____ with the hope that only comes from the promise of your faithful love — your abundant mercy now and the inheritance that is to come.

. . . .

I'm praying Lamentations 3:20–24 for you today, praying that in this difficult time you will experience the mercies of God, the love of God, and the faithfulness of God like never before. I pray that knowing everything you need you have in Christ forever will fill you with hope and joy.

40

I'm praying that you will sing for joy all your days

Teach us to realize the brevity of life,
*   so that we may grow in wisdom ...*
Satisfy us each morning with your unfailing love,
*   so we may sing for joy to the end of our lives.*
Give us gladness in proportion to our former misery!
*   Replace the evil years with good.*

Psalm 90:12, 14–15

At the center of Psalm 90, Moses gives us a petition to bring to God. We are to ask God to teach us to number our days. To put it another way, Moses gives us words to ask for God's help to live in the reality that our days between birth and death are limited. We are not to live foolishly, thinking that we can put off death until it fits into our timetable. Rather, we are to ask God for the wisdom to live in light of the reality of the curse's impact on this world: death. A recognition that we will face death far sooner than we imagine is at the heart of what it means to be wise. This wisdom keeps us from wasting our lives and denying our deaths.

We need perspective about the brevity of this life and the length of the life to come so we won't view our time on earth as all there is. We need the satisfaction that comes from knowing that we are recipients of God's unfailing love every day of our lives, and that the number of days he gives to us is good and right. We need a song to sing on the good days and bad days that will stir up our confidence in God and fill us with rugged joy in spite of pain. We need hope that our lives will not be forever defined by the evil and suffering of this life, but instead will be made radiant with the glory of God into eternity. The psalmist gives us words to ask God to put this song in our hearts in such a way that it will make us truly glad.

. . . .

Prayer

Lord, give _____ the wisdom of a proper perspective about life and death. Satisfy _____ each morning with your unfailing love so that _____ can sing for joy today and every day. Give _____ a song of gladness today and every day!

. . . .

I'm praying Psalm 90 for you today, asking our eternal God to fill you with the kind of wisdom that will enable you to reckon with the brevity of life so that you can sing for joy every day that he gives to you.

Notes

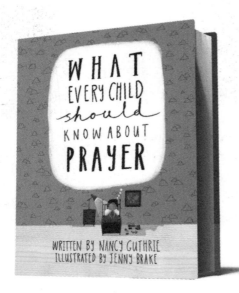

a division of 10 of those.com

10Publishing is the publishing house of **10ofThose**. It is committed to producing quality Christian resources that are biblical and accessible.

www.10ofthose.com is our online retail arm selling thousands of quality books at discounted prices.

For information contact: **info@10ofthose.com** or check out our website: **www.10ofthose.com**